THE THINGS THEY CARRIED

by
Tim O'Brien

Teacher Guide

Written by
Pat Watson

Edited by
Lyn M. Pfordresher

Note
The Broadway Books paperback edition of the book, ©1990 by Tim O'Brien, published 1998, was used to prepare this guide. Page references may differ in other editions.

Please note: This novel deals with sensitive, mature issues. Part may contain profanity, sexual references, and/or descriptions of violence. Please assess the appropriateness of this book for the age level and maturity of your students prior to reading it with them.

ISBN 1-58130-796-9

Printed in the United States of America.

Table of Contents

Skills and Strategies

Comprehension:
Predicting, cause/effect, inference

Literary Elements
Characterization, symbolism, sarcasm, irony, simile, metaphor, theme, acronym

Writing
Poetry, newspaper article, eulogy, epitaph, lament, letter

Listening/Speaking
Discussion, monologue

Vocabulary
Target words, definitions, application

Thinking
Research, compare/contrast, analysis, brainstorming, critical thinking

Across the Curriculum:
Art—collage, montage; Music—ballad; Current Events—magazine/newspaper articles and pictures

Genre: fiction with some factual details

Setting: Vietnam; United States

Point of View: Primarily first person; three chapters are in third-person omniscient

Themes: anxiety; psychological stress; shame/embarrassment; fear; survival; guilt; blame; loneliness; isolation; violence; truth; memory

Conflict: United States vs. Viet Cong; person vs. self; person vs. Government; person vs. person

Style: narrative

Tone: forthright

Summary

Through a series of linked stories, Tim O'Brien provides glimpses of the Vietnam War and those who fought in it. Although the character Tim O'Brien is the narrator, the book is fiction rather than autobiographical, and O'Brien acknowledges that most of the events he records never really happened.

The "things they carry" into the Vietnam War include both tangible and intangible burdens. In addition to the physical necessities for survival, e.g., equipment, weapons, and supplies, they carry cherished mementos, memories, and fears. While in Vietnam, they acquire additional burdens such as guilt, helplessness, anger, and grief. O'Brien reveals the emotional and mental pain the men experience in Vietnam and the nightmarish images they bring home with them.

Honors: National Magazine Award (1987); *New York Times*: named one of ten best books (1990); *Chicago Tribune*: Heartland Award; finalist for Pulitzer Prize and National Book Critics Circle Award; French edition: France's Prix de Meilleur Livre Etranger (1993); selected for inclusion in *Best Short Stories of the Century*, edited by John Updike.

Characters

Members of Alpha Company

Tim O'Brien: the narrator who, in dealing with his own memories, conveys the horrors of the Vietnam War

Jimmy Cross: twenty-four years old; first lieutenant and platoon leader; carries responsibility for his men and blames himself for each death

Ted Lavender: takes tranquilizers to mask his terror; first man to die; memories of his death continue to haunt the others

Mitchell Sanders: kind; devoted to other soldiers; impartial; wants everyone to be treated fairly

Norman Bowker: quiet, introspective; carries emotional scars home with him that culminate in suicide

Bob "Rat" Kiley: platoon's medic; brave and efficient

Kiowa: O'Brien's close friend; compassionate; devout Christian; the horror of his death plagues the others

Henry Dobbins: large man; platoon's machine-gunner

Dave Jensen: minor character

Lee Strunk: minor character; friend of Jensen; dies when he steps on a rigged mortar round

Azar: cruel, unkind; makes crude jokes about death

Curt Lemon: his gruesome death reflects the horrors of war

Others

Elroy Berdahl: eighty-one years old; owns Tip-Top Lodge; prevents O'Brien from defecting to Canada

Mark Fossie: soldier; not part of Cross' platoon; brings his girlfriend to Vietnam

Mary Anne Bell: Fossie's girlfriend; Vietnam turns her innocence into violence

Kathleen: O'Brien's daughter for whom he reveals memories of Vietnam

Background Information

Note: The following information can be used in introductory material, as students read the book, and for post-reading discussion. This information first appeared in the Novel Units® Teacher Guide for *Fallen Angels* by Walter Dean Myers, ©2000.

Vietnam War

The first phase of the war began in 1946 when the Vietnamese fought France for control of Vietnam. After the Vietnamese defeated France in 1954, Vietnam was divided into Communist-ruled North Vietnam and non-Communist South Vietnam. From 1957 to 1965, the war was primarily between the South Vietnamese army and the Viet Cong, Communist-trained South Vietnamese rebels. By late 1964, the Viet Cong controlled about 75 percent of South Vietnam. Beginning in 1965, North Vietnamese regular soldiers and the Viet Cong fought to control South Vietnam; the South Vietnamese army and the United States attempted, but failed to stop them. Thailand, South Korea, the Philippines, Australia, and New Zealand also aided South Vietnam. This was the longest conflict (1957–1975) in which the United States has ever participated, with direct U.S. involvement lasting from 1965–1973.

Important Dates: By 1969: approximately 540,000 U.S. soldiers were involved. 1969: The United States began to withdraw its forces. January 1973: a cease-fire was arranged and the last U.S. ground troops left within two months; fighting soon resumed, but U.S. troops did not return. April 30, 1975: South Vietnam surrendered to North Vietnam, ending the war.

Death and Destruction: About 58,000 Americans were killed and 300,000 wounded. Over 1,000,000 South Vietnamese, between 500,000 and 1,000,000 North Vietnamese, and countless civilians died in the war. An estimated ten million South Vietnamese became refugees, and much of Vietnam lay in ruins.

Other Data: In August 1964 North Vietnamese torpedo boats launched two attacks on U.S. destroyers in the Gulf of Tonkin, and President Lyndon B. Johnson ordered immediate air strikes against Vietnam. He sent the first U.S. combat forces to South Vietnam in March 1965. The first U.S. field commander was General William C. Westmoreland (1964–1968). The United States did not attempt to conquer North Vietnam, but to force them to stop fighting. In the United States, Americans became divided into two groups: the "hawks," who supported the U.S. fight against Communism, and the "doves," who protested U.S. involvement. The United States spent over $150 billion on the Vietnam War.

Aftereffects in the United States: Because this was the first foreign war in which the United States forces failed to achieve their goals, many Americans were left with damaged pride and bitter, painful memories. Returning veterans faced criticism and rejection, and many were left with deep psychological problems. Americans still disagree about whether or not the United States should have been involved in the Vietnam War.

About the Author

Tim O'Brien was born in Austin, Minnesota, on October 1, 1946, and grew up in Worthington, Minnesota. He received a B.A. degree in political science from Macalester College in 1968. He was drafted in 1968 and served with the Third Platoon, A Company, Fifth Battalion, Forty-sixth Infantry, 1969–1970. He received the Purple Heart Award. After being discharged from the military, O'Brien did post-graduate work at Harvard University in 1970. He became a newspaper reporter for the *Washington Post* (1974–75) after interning there as a national affairs reporter. His first book, a war memoir, *If I Die in a Combat Zone, Box Me Up and Send Me Home*" (1973), was named the Outstanding Book of 1973 by the *New York Times*. Other publications include *Northern Lights, Going After Cacciato, The Nuclear Age, In the Lake of the Woods, Tomcat in Love,* and *The Vietnam in Me.*

Initiating Activities

Choose one or more of the following activities to establish an appropriate mindset for the novel.

1. Place the phrase "Vietnam War" on an overhead transparency. Have students brainstorm about their reaction to the phrase: rationale, reactions, personal knowledge, emotions, movies they've seen, books they've read, etc.

2. Display a picture of Picasso's *Guernica*, which was created for the republican government of Spain to commemorate the destruction of the town of Guernica by the Germans. Picasso does not depict the event itself but conveys the general horror and brutality of war. Brainstorm with students what they see in the picture. Note images that reflect brutality and darkness (the bull, severed limbs), the suffering people (horse, man with upraised hands), and the search for hope (girl with the lamp).

3. Read aloud and discuss the following poem: "Dedicated to the Infantryman" by Gary McDonough (**http://grunt.space.swri.edu/infanman.htm**).

4. Preview the book by having students note the author, discuss the title, the cover, the dedication, date of publication, and length of book. Have students make predictions about the book.

5. Have a Vietnam War veteran speak to the class, or invite a panel of three or four veterans to conduct a question/answer open-forum for the class.

6. Research "stream-of-consciousness" writing. Have you ever read a book that includes it? Consider comparing this writing style to that of *Portrait of the Artist as a Young Man* by James Joyce.

Attribute Web

Directions: Record evidence about the narrator, Tim O'Brien (not the author).

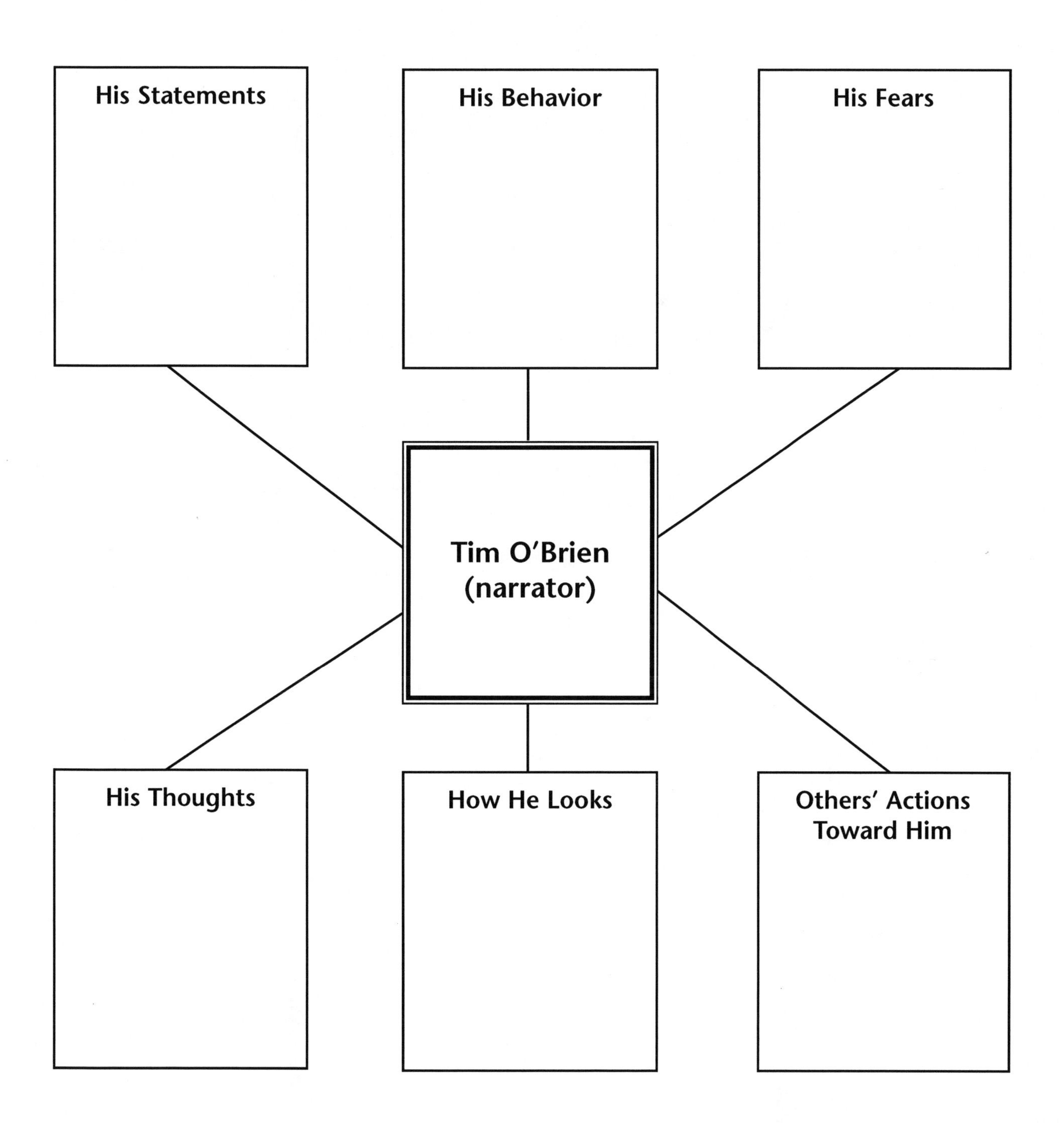

Character Analysis

Directions: Identify and describe the eight men of Alpha Company in the surrounding rectangles, all of the main characters except Tim O'Brien.

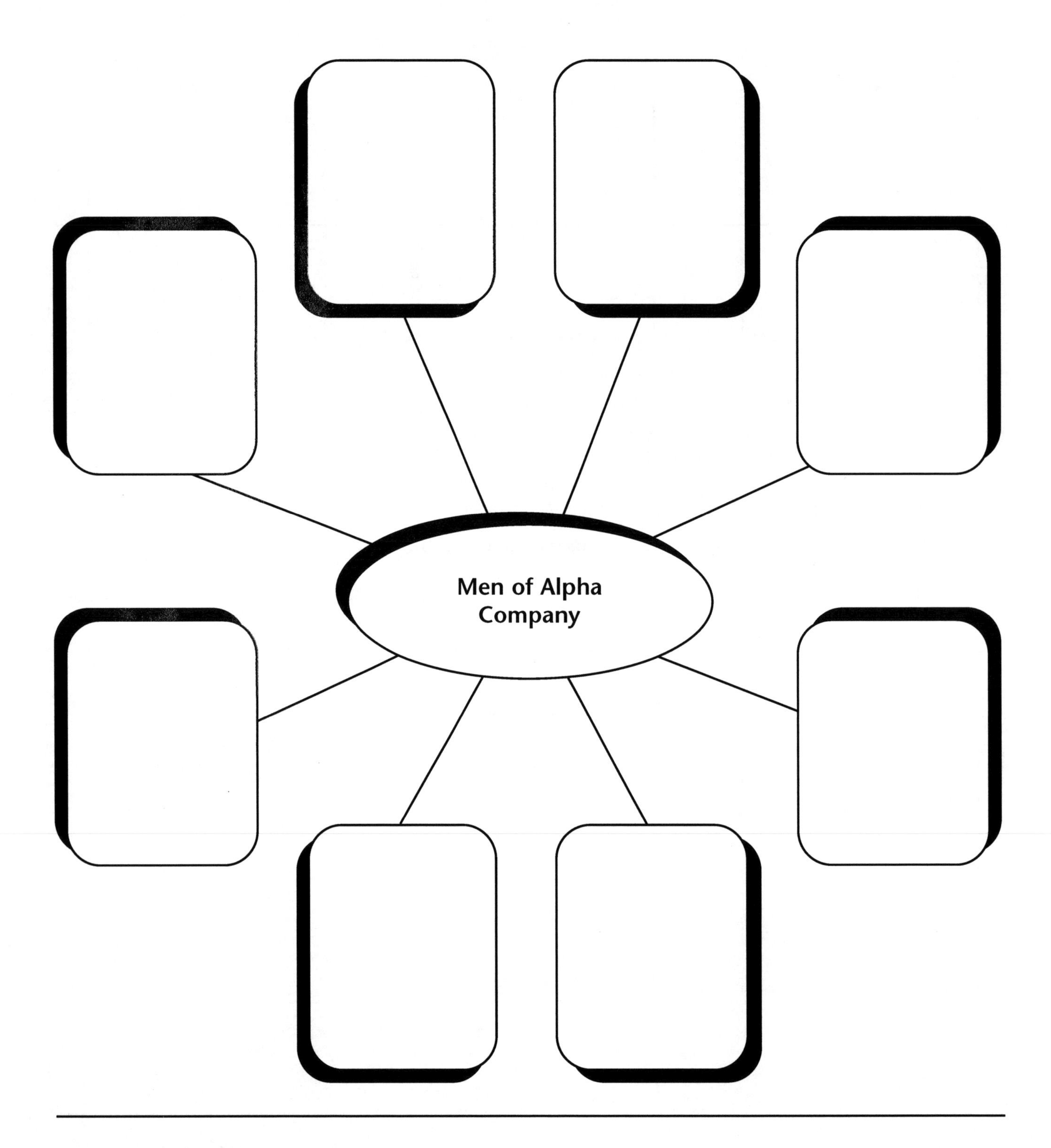

Novel Web Diagram

Directions: The oval is the place for the book's title. Then fill in the boxes to summarize the story.

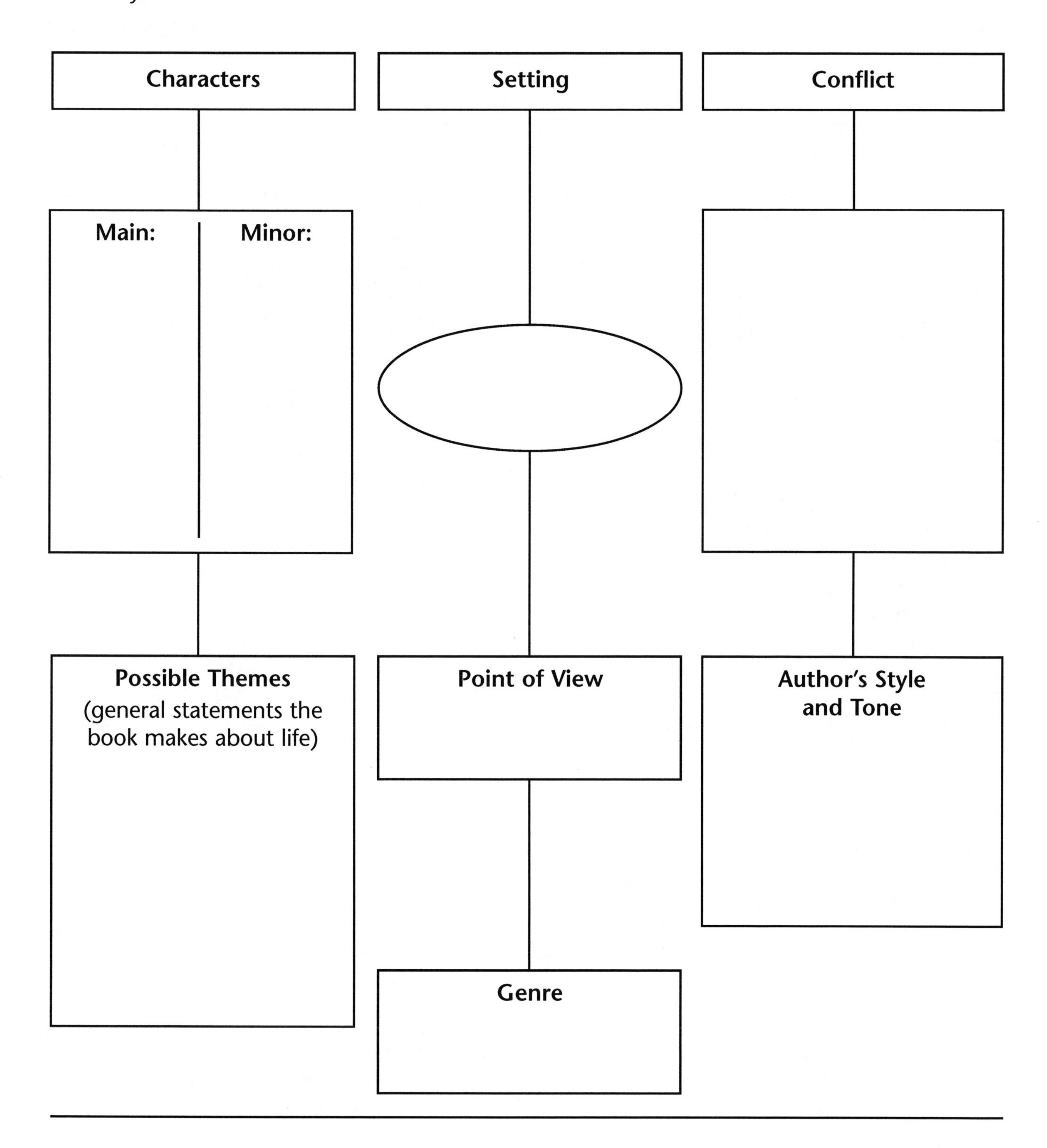

Note: The chapters in the book are unnumbered. Therefore, the discussion questions cover specific pages rather than chapters. A glossary for acronyms and military/slang terms is included in the last section of this guide.

Poetry Patterns

Five-senses: Line 1: color of the emotion; Line 2: sound of the emotion; Line 3: taste of the emotion; Line 4: smell of the emotion; Line 5: sight (what the emotion looks like); Line 6: sensation evoked by the emotion

Metaphor/Simile: Line 1: noun (title); Lines 2–4: something about the subject, each line describing the subject in a different way; Line 5: a metaphor or simile that begins with the noun from line

Name Poem: Place the letters of the name vertically on the paper. Write a descriptive word or phrase beginning with each letter.

Diamente: Line 1: one word (a noun, the subject); Line 2: two words (adjectives that describe line 1); Line 3: three words ("-ing" or "-ed" words that relate to line 1); Line 4: four words (first two relate to line 1; second two relate to line 7); Line 5: three words ("-ing" or "-ed" words that relate to line 7); Line 6: two words (adjectives that describe line 7); Line 7: one word (noun that is the opposite of line 1)

Pages 1–26

First Lieutenant Jimmy Cross leads a platoon of men in the Vietnam War. They each carry physical necessities, war gear, and emotional burdens. Tim Lavender is the first to die.

Vocabulary

metabolism (2) topography (5) volition (15) ambiguities (16)
encyst (20) comport (25)

Acronyms

SOP (2) RTO (3) PRC (5) PFC (5)
KIA (6) AO (9) USO (14)

Military/Slang

rucksack (1) foxhole (1) fatigue (2) flak jacket (3)
to hump (3) grunts (5) platoon (5)
Toe Poppers, Bouncing Betties (9)

Discussion Questions

1. Discuss Lt. Jimmy Cross and what he carries into war. Analyze the significance of his role as leader of the platoon. *(Equipment: compass, maps, code books, binoculars, pistol, strobe light. Personal: pictures of and letters from Martha. Emotional: responsibility for the lives of his men. Significance of his role: he feels the pain and experiences deep guilt when Lavender is killed. This blame/guilt syndrome continues throughout the novel as men under his leadership die. pp. 3–5, 11–12, 16–17, 23–24)*

2. Analyze what Martha symbolizes to Jimmy Cross. *(Memories of her serve as his escape mechanism. Surrounded by war and death, he retreats into an imaginary world where Martha*

returns his love. She also represents regret for what might have been, i.e., if he had been more aggressive in pursuing her, if he had learned her intimate secrets. Thoughts of Martha hinder his ability to concentrate on his responsibilities to his men. He ultimately blames himself for Lavender's death because he had loved Martha more than his men, and he carries this guilt for the rest of the war. His grieving for Lavender becomes intertwined with his grieving for Martha because he realizes she does not love him and never will. He burns her letter and pictures and experiences a love/hate syndrome for her. He becomes hard and determines to exhibit strength and inflexibility toward his men. pp. 4–5, 8–9, 11–12, 16–17, 23–26)

3. Identify the men in Lt. Cross' platoon. Discuss the tangible and intangible burdens each one carries and the common emotional weight all share. *(Tangible: All carry survival necessities, e.g., rations, personal items, water; most carry photographs. Each soldier carries war gear appropriate for his rank and duties and for the specific mission. All carry protective clothing. Mitchell Sanders, RTO, carries the radio; Rat Kily, medic, carries a bag filled with medical supplies; Henry Dobbins, machine gunner, carries an M-60 and ammunition; others, PFCs or Spec 4s, carry rifles and ammunition. Non-military tangibles: Cross—good-luck pebble; Ted Lavender—tranquilizers; Sanders—condoms; Norman Bowker—a diary, thumb from a VC corpse; Kiley—comic books and brandy; Kiowa—New Testament and moccasins; Dave Jensen—night-sight vitamins, rabbit's foot; Lee Strunk—slingshot; Dobbins—his girlfriend's pantyhose; at times they carry each other, the wounded or weak. Intangibles: All carry their own lives and their personal "ghosts," i.e., memories, fear, grief, terror, love, and longing. All carry the common secret of cowardice, for most the heaviest burden of all because they can never put it down, and their reputations depend on their ability to avoid dishonor. Fear of revealing their cowardice causes them to endure, to fight, and sometimes to die. pp. 2–22)*

4. Examine various reactions to Lavender's death and why the men react as they do. Elicit student response concerning different ways of coping with death they have observed or experienced. *(Cross: blames himself, weeps for a long while. Kiowa: feels guilty because he is pleased to be alive. Bowker: reacts in anger when Kiowa won't continue to talk about it. Some tell stories and make jokes about Lavender's use of drugs. Individual reactions reflect the need to escape the reality of death in war and each man's need to hide his own fear of dying. Student responses will vary. Note that people often cope with death by demonstrations of anger, hysterical laughing, denial, mentally "shutting down," stoical acceptance, etc. pp. 16–21)*

5. Analyze the symbolism of the metaphor, "they dreamed of freedom birds" and the ensuing oxymoron, "falling, falling higher and higher." *(The freedom birds are jumbo jets that will carry them away from the war. The men visualize these jets as real birds that will sweep them away from death and allow them to soar above the earth, dropping all their weights and leaving all their burdens behind. They see themselves flying over the Vietnam terrain and over their own familiar regions in America. Falling higher indicates their desire to fall away from the terror of Vietnam, even to the edge of the earth, then rising into the weightlessness and nothingness of space. Only there will they be free of the burdens they carry. pp. 22–23)*

6. **Prediction**: Have students write down the names of men in Cross' platoon they think will survive the war.

Supplementary Activities

1. Have students (a) write a letter from Jimmy Cross to Martha after he burns her letters and pictures or (b) write a five-senses poem, "Guilt," reflecting Jimmy Cross' reaction to Lavender's death.

2. Have students begin a list of literary devices in the novel. Examples: **Metaphor**—Imagination: a killer (p. 11); resupply choppers: great American war chest (p. 16) **Similes**— They moved like moles (p. 15); They (soldiers) carried (their burdens) like freight trains (p. 16); This (memory of Lavender's death) was something he (Cross) would have to carry like a stone in his stomach for the rest of the war (p. 16).

Pages 27–38

Several years after the war, O'Brien and Cross reminisce about the things they still carry. O'Brien relates stories from the war.

Vocabulary

antipersonnel (36) lethal (37)

Acronyms

AWOL (35)

Military/Slang

poppa-san (33) dink (33) body bag (37)

Discussion Questions

1. Discuss the switch from third person to first person. Elicit student response concerning why the author uses this technique. *(Responses will vary. Ideas: O'Brien veers from the more objective third-person omniscient to a personal first-person approach. This emphasizes the lapse of time and the retrospective memories of Vietnam. Although he is now 43 years old, the memories he and Jimmy Cross share are as vivid as the day they happened. pp. 27–28)*

2. Examine the memories O'Brien and Cross share and what these reveal about the two men. *(Through old pictures and stories, their buddies who died in Vietnam will remain forever young. They are able to laugh about some of the craziness of men in war. Cross reveals that he has never forgiven himself for Lavender's death. After showing O'Brien a picture of Martha, Cross tells of their reunion. O'Brien learns that Martha has become a Lutheran missionary. Cross vows his continuing love for Martha, but acknowledges that she never had any romantic interest in him. His final request reveals his desire to be remembered as the best platoon leader ever and alludes to his guilt over Lavender's death. Memories of the Vietnam War remain vivid for both men. pp. 27–30)*

3. Analyze the contradictions of war O'Brien reveals in "Spin": terror and violence vs. sweetness, gentleness, humor, and monotony. Elicit responses as to what they consider the most poignant memory. *(Terror/violence: Kiowa sinking into a field of human waste and mud; Curt Lemon hanging in pieces from a tree; the death of a young Vietnamese soldier; tense boredom, waiting for gunfire; the smell of an empty body bag; Azar strapping Lavender's puppy to a mine. Sweetness and gentleness: Bowker and Dobbins playing checkers; Azar giving candy to a maimed*

Vietnamese child; the old Vietnamese man guiding the platoon through the minefields; Bowker's wishing for a letter from his father telling him it's okay if he doesn't win any medals; Kiowa teaching a rain dance to Kiley and Jensen; Lavender adopting an orphan puppy. Humor: Lavender's reaction to tranquilizers; Dobbins' singing as he sews on his stripes; Sanders' tales. Monotony: digging foxholes, slapping mosquitoes; Answers will vary. pp. 31–37)

4. O'Brien remembers the checker game having "something restful about it." How does the game contrast to the Vietnam War? *(The playing field was a strict grid; you knew the score; the enemy was visible; there was a winner and a loser. p. 32)*

Supplementary Activities

1. Have students write a metaphor or simile poem based on O'Brien's explanation of stories. (Remembering and retelling a story takes it from the past and places it in the present. Stories join the past to the future. "Stories are for eternity." p. 38)
2. Have students add two similes and one metaphor to their list of literary devices. Examples: **Metaphor**—memories: traffic (p. 34) **Similes**—war was like a Ping-Pong ball (p. 32); you could end up like popcorn (p. 33); feel boredom dripping inside you like a leaky faucet (p. 34); things often took on a curiously playful atmosphere like a sporting event (p. 37)

Pages 39–66

O'Brien is drafted into the Vietnam War. He attempts to defect to Canada but changes his mind after an encounter with Elroy Berdahl. In Vietnam, tensions build between members of the platoon.

Vocabulary

amortizing (40)	liberal (42)	hawk (42)	eviscerated (42)
deferments (43)	pacifist (44)	schizophrenia (44)	acquiescence (45)
platitudes (45)	cryptic (49)	reticence (51)	impassive (60)

Acronyms

SEATO (40	CO (44)	FBI (50)	LZ (62)

Military/Slang

dustoff (66)

Discussion Questions

1. Examine why O'Brien has never told the story "On the Rainy River" and why he now decides to do so. *(Responses will vary; Ideas: he has always thought the story would cause embarrassment. The memory still bothers him, and he decides to tell the story, hoping to relieve the pressure of his dreams. When O'Brien's draft notice arrives in 1968, he discovers that he is a coward rather than the hero he had assumed he would be. His narrative reveals his inward conflict and its ultimate resolution. This is an example of one type of literary catharsis, i.e., writing to relieve and correct an unhealthy emotional state produced by conflicting feelings. pp. 39–61)*
2. Examine O'Brien's reaction to the Vietnam War in 1968 and his response to the draft notice. *(He hates the war and cannot understand the rationale for fighting. He believes you do not make war without knowing why. He participates in mild protests, e.g., ringing doorbells for McCarthy*

and writing a few uninspired editorials for the campus newspaper. He feels no personal danger until his draft notice arrives. The notice creates within him a silent "howl," and he feels he is too good for the war and there must be a mistake. He is a liberal and has just graduated from college with high honors, with a scholarship for graduate studies at Harvard. He hates dirt, tents, mosquitoes, blood, and authority. Therefore, how can he become a soldier? His emotions change from rage to self-pity to numbness. pp. 40–42)

3. Discuss O'Brien's summer job and analyze why he gives such a graphic description of his work. *(He works at a meatpacking plant. The pigs are slaughtered, decapitated, split and pried open, eviscerated, and then strung by the hocks on a conveyor belt. O'Brien then removes blood clots from the neck of the pigs. He compares his job to standing for eight hours a day under a "lukewarm blood-shower." The stink never leaves him, and he feels isolated. He sums up the experience by saying that life seems to be collapsing toward slaughter, symbolizing his visions of heading for the slaughter of Vietnam. pp. 42–43, 53)*

4. Examine the options for avoiding being drafted for the Vietnam War and how they apply to O'Brien. *(The government has ended most graduate school deferments and there are long waiting lists for the National Guard and Reserves. O'Brien is in good health, and cannot apply for Conscientious Objector status because he has no religious grounds or history as a pacifist. The only option he thinks is available to him is to defect to Canada. pp. 43–44)*

5. Analyze O'Brien's struggle with the decision to escape to Canada and the ensuing results. *(He experiences emotional conflict over the decision and encounters a myriad of emotions. He doesn't believe in the war and he doesn't want to die. He fears war, yet he fears exile, i.e., losing the respect of his parents, being pursued by the law. He blames the community for their complacency and lack of understanding of the war, but he fears public ridicule and censure as a defector. The emotions of outrage, terror, bewilderment, guilt, and sorrow overpower him, and he finally "cracks." He walks out of the packing plant and drives north. He takes off with no plan and reaches the Tip Top Lodge, a fishing resort on Rainy River; the next stop is Canada. pp. 44–48)*

6. Characterize Elroy Berdahl and analyze his influence on O'Brien. Discuss O'Brien's physical and mental reactions while he is at Tip Top Lodge. *(Berdahl is skinny, shrunken, almost bald, and eighty-one years old. His eyes pierce through O'Brien with a cutting sensation, and he recognizes that this is a kid in trouble. He owns the Tip Top Lodge, and O'Brien stays there for six days. During this time, Berdahl does not probe into O'Brien's problem but just becomes a friend to him. O'Brien's physical reactions: vomiting, sweats, is dizzy with sorrow, can't sleep or lie still. Mental reactions: thinks he's gone off the psychic edge, can't tell up from down, experiences weird pictures spinning through his head, imagines he is being chased by the border Patrol. He opens up and talks to Berdahl about the gory job in the packing plant. He believes Berdahl knows about his plans. O'Brien credits Berdahl with bringing him to the point of choosing between going to war and fleeing to Canada. pp. 48–56)*

7. Analyze O'Brien's sense of shame and his final decision about defecting. *(Shame: doesn't want people to think badly of him; ashamed of his conscience; ashamed to do the right thing, escape to Canada. When he is 20 yards from freedom in Canada, he confronts his moral dilemma. A "moral freeze" grips his heart, and he cries, unable to decide or to comport himself with human dignity. He realizes that Canada is a pitiful fantasy. He chooses not to do what he should do, flee*

from the war, because he can't risk the embarrassment. He will go to war, will kill, and maybe die, because he is embarrassed not to. In retrospect, he says that he went to war because he was a coward. pp. 56–61)

8. Introduce the stream-of-consciousness concept and correlate it with the statement, "Chunks of my own history flashed by" (p. 57). *(Stream-of-consciousness: the freely flowing thoughts, memories, reflections, and associations of any one of the characters in a story; these may seem disjointed and illogical. O'Brien sees himself in disjointed segments of his life, from childhood to future, including people, places, and events. Note that the book was written many years after the war, allowing the author to portray future events as well as past and present. Some of these memories are associated with the author himself, others with the fictitious O'Brien. pp. 57–58)*

9. Analyze elements of the conflict and resolution between Lee Strunk and Dave Jensen that reflect the tensions in Vietnam. Be sure to include the pact they make. *(In the tenseness of war, men fight over frivolous things but must reconcile quickly because their lives may depend on each other in the next battle. Jensen and Strunk fight over a missing jackknife. Jensen breaks Strunk's nose, then becomes worried that Strunk will come after him with a gun. Jensen starts firing randomly, then breaks his own nose to "square" things with Strunk. The two men reconcile their differences, learn to trust each other, team up on ambushes, and make a pact to kill the other if he gets "messed up." When Strunk steps on a mine that takes away most of his leg, he is afraid Jensen will kill him. Jensen consoles Strunk, but seems relieved when Strunk dies. pp. 62–66)*

Supplementary Activities

1. Have students write (a) a poem beginning with "I stood at the crossroads..." or (b) a short essay in which they support or refute the statement beginning, "Courage comes to us in finite quantities..." (p. 40).

2. Have students add three similes to their list. Examples: I sometimes felt the fear spreading inside me like weeds (p. 44); The main building...seemed to lean heavily to one side like a cripple (p. 48); He was a witness, like God, or like the gods (p. 60). See also pp. 43, 47, 54, 57, 62, 65.

Pages 67–88

O'Brien gives his definition for a true war story. Curt Lemon's death and the ensuing events illustrate the horror of war.

Vocabulary

villes (68)	rectitude (68)	surreal (71)	napalm (75)
ordnance (75)	aesthetic (81)	anarchy (82)	trite (83)
sadism (87)			

Acronyms

LP (72)	VC (78)

Discussion Questions

1. Examine O'Brien's criteria for a true war story. Elicit responses as to whether or not the stories Kiley and Sanders tell fit these criteria. *(A true war story is never moral, doesn't instruct or teach a virtue, will contain absolute and uncompromising allegiance to obscenity and evil, will embarrass the listener, tries to make fun, never seems to end, does not generalize, makes the stomach believe, often doesn't even have a point, and nothing is absolutely true. Responses will vary. Ideas—Kiley's story: doesn't teach a moral, includes references to obscenity and evil, alludes to making war fun, doesn't make the reader feel uplifted. Sanders' story: has a moral, i.e. nobody listens; he admits part of it is fabricated. pp. 67–85)*

2. Discuss the story of Curt Lemon's death. Elicit student reaction to the story and analyze why O'Brien says this story "makes his stomach believe." *(Lemon and Kiley are goofing off as they hike through the jungle. They begin to play a game of "chicken" they invented, catching grenades from which they have pulled the pins. A booby trap explodes just as Lemon steps into the sunlight, blowing him into a tree. Jensen and O'Brien must retrieve the body parts from the tree. The sickening sight of the body parts in the tree make O'Brien ill, thus his stomach believes. pp. 69–71, 82–84)*

3. Examine the cause and effect of the death of the water buffalo, and analyze what the deaths of Lemon and the water buffalo symbolize. *(Cause: Curt Lemon's death. Effect: later that day, the men find and rope a water buffalo in the mountain. At first Kily strokes the animal's nose, then begins to shoot it repeatedly and mercilessly. Kiley begins to cry when the animal is almost dead and goes away by himself. Someone else kicks the barely living animal, then others dump the body in a well. The combination of grief and rage symbolizes the horror of war. pp. 78–80, 85)*

4. Analyze the metaphor "Vietnam is the Garden of Evil." Note the statement, "...every sin's real fresh and original. "Correlate with the Biblical story of the Garden of Eden (Genesis 2–4). *(Because of the war, evil has invaded Vietnam. Otherwise peaceful, gentle people become killers and discover they are capable of vicious deeds they would never have imagined. Fear is ever present, the land is often barren, and the gore of war is everywhere. Nothing will ever be quite the same as pre-war Vietnam. In the Garden of Eden, everything was perfect, and man had everything he needed. The entry of evil through the first sin caused fear, barrenness, isolation, and murder. Humankind survived, but life had changed forever. In the "Garden of Evil," war is another name for death. In the Garden of Eden, sin was another name for death. pp. 80–81)*

5. Analyze the ambiguities of war and why truths about it are contradictory. *(War contradictions: War is hell but is also mystery, terror, adventure, courage, holiness, pity, despair, longing, and love. In war almost everything is true, yet almost nothing is true. It makes you a man, but also makes you dead; you are never more alive than when you're almost dead. War is: nasty/fun; thrilling/drudgery; ugliness/beauty; right/wrong; order/chaos; love/hate; law/anarchy; civility/savagery. Depending on the time, the place, and the circumstances, war can be anything the participant feels it to be, yet any of these factors can cause everything to change in an instant. pp. 80–82)*

6. Characterize Curt Lemon and discuss why O'Brien places "The Dentist" after the story of Lemon's death. *(Lemon: tries to play the tough soldier; replays his exploits with embellishments to alleviate either high or low self-esteem; is deathly afraid of being in the dentist's chair. It is easy to get sentimental over death and build a person into a paragon of virtue. The story of Lemon's fear*

of the dentist, his passing out, and then returning and having the dentist pull a healthy tooth portrays Lemon as he really was: a human with frailties, but a soldier for whom they grieve. pp. 86–88)

Supplementary Activities

1. Have (a) students write a name poem for Curt Lemon or (b) write a poem beginning with the phrase, "War is hell..."

2. Have students add one simile and two metaphors to their list. Examples: **Simile**—It's (moral to a war story) like the thread that makes the cloth (p. 77). **Metaphors**—War: hell (p. 78); Vietnam: Garden of Evil (p. 80)

Pages 89–116

The "Sweetheart of the Song Tra Bong," Mary Anne Bell, comes to Vietnam to be with her boyfriend. The war transforms her from an innocent, lovely young girl into a dangerous, bloodthirsty fighter.

Vocabulary

mundane (89)	superlatives (90)	imprecision (99)	opaque (105)
digressions (107)	endorphins (114)		

Acronyms

NCO (91)	RF (91)	PF (91)	ARVN (91)
R&R (113)	MP (115)	CID (115)	

Military/Slang

boonies (90)	Green Berets (92)	Ruff-and-Puffs (91)	mama-san (93)

Discussion Questions

1. Discuss the story of Mary Anne Bell and apply the criteria of a true war story to this tale. *(Seventeen-year-old Mary Anne comes to Vietnam to be with Mark Fossie, her boyfriend. Initially, they are happy to be together, but she gradually becomes intrigued with the war and the country. She enjoys being involved with all aspects of the war, has no fear, and quickly falls into the habits of the bush. She withdraws further and further from Mark. True war story criteria that apply: doesn't instruct, contains obscenity and evil, has elements that embarrass the listener, makes war fun, has no definitive ending, makes the stomach believe, does not generalize, and has no definitive ending. The story does have a moral, i.e., war changes everyone whose life it touches. pp. 93–94, 98–114)*

2. Analyze the changes in Mary Anne and what these changes symbolize. *(When she first arrives in Vietnam, she is in love with Mark and full of dreams for their future. She is intelligent, attractive, bubbly, and friendly. Her intrigue with the war and Vietnam becomes the focal point of her life. She undergoes a transformation physically, mentally, and emotionally. She no longer attends to her physical appearance and is not intimidated by blood or fear. She learns how to assemble and use weapons and becomes confident and authoritarian. Although she continues to profess her love for Mark, she becomes vague about their future plans. She begins to disappear for hours, Mark discovers she has gone on ambush with the Green Berets when she fails to return one night.*

After briefly acquiescing to Mark's demands to stay in camp, she finally leaves with the "Greenies." She eventually returns, but has physically and mentally become one in spirit with Vietnam, participating in rituals associated with the hunt and the kill of war. She eventually walks away into the mountains and never comes back. Mary Anne's transformation is summarized in the statement, "What happened to her...was what happened to all of them. You come over clean and you get dirty and then afterward it's never the same," p. 114. The changes in Mary Ann symbolize the effect of Vietnam on the innocence and dreams of those who were sent into the war. pp. 89–116)

3. Introduce the concept of literary sarcasm: a form of verbal irony in which, under the guise of praise, the author presents a caustic and bitter expression of personal disapproval. Note the sarcasm when Kiley says of Mary Anne, "Well hey, she'll make a sweet bride...Combat ready" (p. 103). Elicit responses as to what the author is actually saying. *(Responses will vary. Ideas: Fossie's skepticism about Mary Anne's ability to forget the war and become a "sweet bride" reflects the author's cynicism about the ability of Vietnam veterans to forget the war and settle into a well-adjusted civilian life.)*

4. Analyze the metaphors on page 107: military forces: zoo; soldiers: animals. *(Responses will vary. Ideas: The author presents the military forces as one big zoo, with the "animals" expected to conform and perform while their "keepers"—commanders and political forces—command them. The soldiers lose their individuality in their struggle to survive. They become more like animals than humans.)*

Supplementary Activities

1. Have students (a) draw a caricature of Mary Anne as a combat-ready bride or (b) write two name poems for Mary Anne Bell, one before and one after her transformation.

2. Have students add three similes and two metaphors to their list. Examples: **Similes**—(Mary Anne) complexion like strawberry ice cream (p. 93). The seven silhouettes seemed to float across the surface of the earth, like spirits...(p. 105). (Mary Anne) seemed to flow like water...like oil (p. 115). See also pp. 92, 96, 109, 111. **Metaphor**—Greenies (Green Berets): animals (p. 92). See also those on p. 107.

Pages 117–136

O'Brien reveals characteristics and eccentricities of the men in his platoon. He is haunted by memories of the man he killed.

Vocabulary

eccentricity (117)	talisman (118)	pagoda (119)	cadres (128)
piasters (129)	hamlet (135)		

Military/Slang

didi mau (122)

Discussion Questions

1. Examine what this section reveals about the characteristics and eccentricities of Dobbins, Kiowa, Azar, and O'Brien. *(Dobbins: superstitious; believes a pair of his girlfriend's pantyhose is his good luck charm, they are like body armor, keeping him safe; he stereotypes ministers as having many "freebies"; believes in God, but isn't religious; wants to become a minister because he wants to be nice to people, even though he does not feel smart enough for the sermons; Kiowa: deeply religious; believes establishing a fortress in a church is sacrilegious and is "bad news"; rationalizes the death of the enemy; consoles those who are troubled; Azar: makes crude jokes about the men who die; mockingly cruel, e.g., mimics the Vietnamese girl who loses her family; O'Brien: deeply troubled when he kills a man. throughout section)*

2. Analyze the symbolism of the monks' repetitive motion of washing of their hands. Correlate with the phrase, "I wash my hands of this." *(Based on the story of Pilate washing his hands as a symbol of his innocence in the death of Jesus Christ (Matthew 27:25), washing of the hands symbolizes a person's innocence in perpetrating an evil deed or something about which s/he does not approve. When the Americans first dig foxholes in the yard of the pagoda, the younger monk performs the washing motion with his hands. Although the monks do not seem displeased with the Americans' presence and assist them, they are "washing their hands" of the death and destruction of the war. Dobbins mimics the monks when they leave the pagoda. pp. 119–123)*

3. Discuss O'Brien's speculation about the background of the man he killed and analyze why he does so. Note the number of times he mentions the man's eye, now a star-shaped hole, and the significance of the repetition. *(By the man's physical appearance, O'Brien recognizes the man's youth and lack of physical prowess. He thinks the young man might have been a scholar who became a soldier because of his love for Vietnam, not because he was a Communist. This leads O'Brien to speculate about his birth date, where he had lived, his training as a loyal citizen, and his desire for the war to end. He believes the man hated violence but pretended to look forward to doing his patriotic duty because he feared disgracing himself. He envisions the young man falling in love, even though he knew he would die in the war. Through his speculation, O'Brien makes the man a person rather than an enemy who had to be destroyed, thus putting a "face" to the war. The star-shaped hole that replaces an eye troubles O'Brien because "the light of life is in the eye," and the light is now extinguished. pp. 124–128)*

4. Examine the effect of the man's death on O'Brien and the way in which Kiowa consoles him. *(O'Brien stares at the body, unable to leave the scene. He reflects that he did not hate the young man or see him as the enemy, yet he killed him. When the young man appeared out of the fog, O'Brien was terrified and threw the grenade that killed him. O'Brien later believes he was in no peril, and that the man would have passed by. He still struggles with forgiving himself and occasionally "sees" the young man again, passing by and fading into the fog. Kiowa consoles O'Brien by telling him he did what he had to do and that the young man would have killed him. Kiowa rationalizes by telling O'Brien it was a good kill, that he is a solder and this is war, and that he should shape up, stop staring, and move on. pp. 126–134)*

5. Discuss how the young Vietnamese girl copes with death. Elicit student response concerning different ways people cope with death. *(Her house and most of the hamlet have been burned, and her family is dead and badly burned. She copes by dancing, sometimes smiling to herself dreamily. She puts her hands against her ears as if to shut out the sounds of death. Responses will*

vary. Ideas: people develop their own defense mechanisms such as retreating into their own world, isolating themselves from others, constantly being busy, reliving the dead person's life through stories, etc. pp. 135–136)

Supplementary Activities

1. Have students write a diamente poem contrasting life and death.
2. Have students add two similes to their list. Examples: They (pantyhose) were like body armor (p. 118); cowlick that rose up like a bird's tail at the back of his head (p. 129)

Pages 137–161

Norman Bowker reminisces about the Vietnam War. He longs to tell someone about the horror of Kiowa's death. Bowker eventually commits suicide.

Vocabulary

affluent (138)	valor (140)	irony (146)	catharsis (157)
metaphoric (159)	virtues (160)	anthology (160)	complicity (160)

Acronyms

GI (145)

Discussion Questions

1. Analyze the aftereffects of the war on Norman Bowker. *(He is constantly in motion but feels he is in no hurry because he has nowhere to go. He repeatedly drives around the lake, which represents his life before the war. He remembers driving around the lake with his high school girlfriend, who is now married, and his friend who drowned in the lake. Regardless of what he is doing, thoughts of the war press on his mind intermittently, especially flashbacks about Kiowa's death, for which he feels responsible. He imagines talking to his father about Kiowa's death, yet knows he could never talk about it. He thinks he had not been as brave as he wanted to be, despite how brave he was over all. He had let Kiowa go. pp. 137–154)*
2. Examine Bowker's thoughts after he returns from the Vietnam War: what might have been, what he wishes for, and what he finds. *(He thinks that, if he had not gone to war, he might have married Sally Kramer, but she is married when he returns. He wants to share his intuition for time with her, something he learned as a soldier. He wants to tell his father why he did not receive the Silver Star, but Bowker believes that no one in town wants to hear about the horror of war; instead they want to hear about good deeds. pp. 138–141, 155–156)*
3. Discuss the medals Bowker received, and analyze why he keeps referring to the medal he did not receive. *(Received 7 medals: Combat Infantryman's Badge, Air Medal [meritorious achievement in flight], Army Commendation Medal [meritorious service], Good Conduct Medal, Vietnam Campaign Medal, Bronze Star [heroic or meritorious achievement during military operations], Purple Heart [wounded in combat]. He did not receive the Silver Star, given for uncommon valor in action. He blames himself for Kiowa's death and believes he could have exhibited uncommon valor that night. After Kiowa was hit by enemy fire and began to slip into the field of mud and human waste, Bowker caught hold of his boot but let him go because of the*

filth and horrible smell. If he had saved Kiowa's life, he would have received the Silver Star. It is Kiowa's death, not the medal, that haunts him. pp. 141–149)

4. Discuss why Bowker writes to O'Brien and the effect of the letter on O'Brien. *(He explains to O'Brien how meaningless his life has become since Vietnam. He explains that he has read O'Brien's first book,* If I Die in a Combat Zone, *and liked it except for the political parts. He then tells O'Brien that he should write a story about a guy [Bowker] who can never get his act together because he is haunted by Kiowa's death and wants to talk about it but can't. Effect: The letter disrupts O'Brien's feeling of smugness about how easily he has adjusted to life after the war. He believes his writing has been a catharsis for him by explaining what happened and why. Yet, Bowker's letter makes him realize his stories contain some truths, but also some fabrications. The letter haunts him, and he includes a chapter about Bowker in the book he is writing. He feels he has provided Bowker a voice in the story, yet he changes the horrible circumstances of Kiowa's death, replacing the real story with one that better fits his book. pp. 157–159)*

5. Discuss why Bowker commits suicide. *(Responses will vary. Ideas: He has difficulty finding a meaningful use for his life after the war, and his life as a returning veteran is almost like he was killed in Vietnam. He has no place to go and is consumed with self-pity, anger, and guilt. He blames himself for Kiowa's death and is unable to forget the horrible circumstances of it. pp. 155–157)*

Supplementary Activities

1. Have students write a letter from Bowker to his father explaining Bowker's need for someone to listen to him and explain why he didn't receive the Silver Star.
2. Have students add one simile to their list: Her eyes were as fluffy and airy-light as cotton candy (p. 151).

Pages 162–188

The men of the platoon search for Kiowa's body, blaming themselves for his death. O'Brien returns to Vietnam twenty years later, searching for closure.

Vocabulary

latrine (166)	tactically (169)	elusive (170)	condolences (176)

Acronyms

MIA (163)	LT (166)

Discussion Questions

1. Discuss O'Brien's reflections on the night of Kiowa's death and compare/contrast it with Bowker's version. *(O'Brien explains that it was he, not Bowker, who failed the night of Kiowa's death. By switching to the third-person omniscient voice in "In the Field," O'Brien relates how Cross and a young soldier [O'Brien] both feel responsible for the death. Cross, as commanding officer, blames himself because of his failure to follow his first impulse and not set up camp on the edge of the river. The young soldier [O'Brien] blames himself because he switched on his flashlight to show Kiowa a picture of his girlfriend; the flashlight made a perfect target. He remembers Kiowa*

being hit, ducking under the water, then grabbing Kiowa's boot, but finally letting it go. O'Brien's and Bowker's stories both give details of Kiowa's being hit by enemy fire and sinking into the slime. In his reflections, Bowker blames himself for letting go of Kiowa's boot. In "In the Field," Azar feels guilty because of his insensitive and crude jokes; Bowker declares that the death is "Nobody's fault...Everybody's." pp. 161–176)

2. Analyze the metaphors (p. 167) that compare the field where Kiowa is lost to a golf course, Kiowa to a lost ball, and the members of the platoon to tired players. *(After Kiowa's death, the men begin searching for his body in the slimy water. The water is deep and extensive [like a water hazard in the rough of a golf course], Kiowa is lost [like a golf ball in the rough], and the men [those who had played the "game"] must sweep back and forth in a systematic pattern until they find him. In the game of golf, however, the players lose a ball, never a player.)*

3. Analyze the difference between story truth and happening truth. *(O'Brien states that story truth is sometimes truer than happening truth. Story truth makes things present, allows the author to attach faces to emotions he felt in Vietnam, allows him to be brave, and makes him feel again. "Happening" truth: he is 43 years old, a writer, and a long time ago he was a foot soldier in Vietnam; he saw real bodies with real faces but was afraid to look; he now feels faceless responsibility and faceless grief. He acknowledges that he has invented almost everything else in his stories of Vietnam. Two versions of "Story" truth: [1] twenty years before he watched a man die near the village of My Khe; he did not kill him but his presence made him guilty; [2] he killed a young Vietnamese man and remembers the star-shaped hole where an eye had been. pp. 179–180)*

4. Examine O'Brien's search for and discovery of closure for his part in the Vietnam War. *(He returns to Vietnam with his ten-year-old daughter Kathleen. She asks many unanswerable questions about her father's involvement in the war, and he tells her he just wanted to stay alive. She thinks it is weird that he can't forget. They visit the site of Kiowa's death, where O'Brien searches for closure. The field where Kiowa died is now bone dry except for a few marshy spots, and it is smaller and not as menacing as O'Brien remembers. No ghosts remain, and the place is at peace. He takes a few pictures and mentally relives the night Kiowa died. He acknowledges to himself that this field embodies for him all the waste, the vulgarity, and the horror of Vietnam. Here he lost his best friend, his pride, and his belief in himself as a man of dignity and courage. At first he fails to feel any real emotion, but he finds closure by going into the slimy water at the river's edge and placing Kiowa's moccasins into the muck. For O'Brien, the war is finally over. pp. 181–188)*

Supplementary Activities

1. Have students work in small groups and research Post-Traumatic Stress Disorder, then prepare a chart comparing the symptoms with those Bowker and O'Brien experience after the war.

2. Have students add two similes and two metaphors to their list. Examples: **Similes**—The rain made quick dents in the water like tiny mouths (p. 165); the field seemed to pull back like a tug-of-war he couldn't win (p. 171). See also p. 187. **Metaphor**—Kiowa: lost golf ball (p. 167) (See question #2 in this section.)

Pages 189–218

O'Brien is shot twice, and the medic who tends him the second time almost lets him die. He seeks revenge against the medic when he next encounters him.

Vocabulary

gangrene (190)	tempo (193)	tic (201)	levitate (202)
rapport (203)	coherence (209)	atrocity (209)	resonance (210)
inflection (212)	wistful (212)	lucid (214)	

Military/Slang

stand-down (193)	klicks (195)	Charlie Cong (202)	bunker (204)

Discussion Questions

1. Discuss O'Brien's war injuries and why he wants revenge from Bobby Jorgenson. *(Rat Kiley is the medic when O'Brien is first injured. He thanks God for Kiley, whose quick attention and encouragement prevent shock and infection. He returns to the platoon 26 days later. Bobby Jorgenson, who is green, incompetent, and scared, has replaced Kiley, who was wounded. When O'Brien is shot the second time, he almost dies from shock because of Jorgenson's slow response, and he develops an infection because of Jorgenson's inept treatment. After the second injury, O'Brien is transferred to a battalion supply section. As he slowly recovers, he plots revenge against Jorgenson. pp. 189–193)*

2. Examine O'Brien's reaction to being reassigned away from the heat of battle and what happens when the men from Alpha Company return to base. *(He feels fairly safe for the first time in months, yet at times he misses the adventure and danger of the battlefield and the camaraderie of the other men in the platoon. When Alpha Company returns, O'Brien feels isolated from the men, as if he has forfeited membership in the group. He becomes the brunt of some jokes about the injury to his buttocks. Even as he listens to tales from the battlefield, he continues to be consumed with desire for revenge against Jorgenson. He feels betrayed when Sanders tells him to forget revenge and assures him that Jorgenson is now "with them," i.e., a vital part of the platoon. pp. 193–198)*

3. Discuss O'Brien's meeting with Jorgenson and O'Brien and Azar's plan for revenge against Jorgenson. *(The two men meet and Jorgenson apologizes and explains his perception of what happened. O'Brien refuses to shake his hand. Azar and O'Brien agree to spook Jorgenson when he is on guard duty by rigging flares, ropes, rattles made of ammo cans filled with rifle cartridges, tear-gas grenades, and sandbags. O'Brien tries to retreat from their plan, but Azar is determined to proceed. Their psychological attack becomes gradually more aggressive, and Jorgenson eventually begins to fire at the sandbag but does not "go nuts." He realizes O'Brien is the instigator and calls out his name. O'Brien has gotten revenge but finds no satisfaction in having done so. Azar, disgusted with O'Brien, kicks him in the head and leaves. O'Brien and Jorgenson agree they are even and shake hands. pp. 198–218)*

4. Analyze the metaphor that identifies the "ghost" in Vietnam. *(Charlie Cong, i.e., the Viet Cong, is the main ghost. To the Americans, to get spooked means to get killed. It seems as if the land is haunted and the men are fighting an unseen, evil force that appears and disappears almost magically. "He," the enemy, comes out silently at night, and the men never really see him but*

think they do. The men believe Charlie Cong can levitate, fly, pass through barbed wire, and melt away like ice. p. 202)

5. Examine how O'Brien has changed during the war. *(When he entered the war, he was quiet and thoughtful. He had graduated from college with high honors and high hopes for his future. Seven months in the bush have crushed his civilized, hopeful view of life. He has turned mean inside and can sometimes be cruel. He feels cold inside, realizes he is capable of evil, and has become vindictive against anyone who harms him. p. 200)*

Supplementary Activities

1. Have students research near-death experiences. In a class discussion, correlate with O'Brien's description of his experience after he was shot near the Song Tra Bong River (pp. 213–214).

2. Have students add two similes and three metaphors to their list. Examples: **Similes**—It (the desire to get even) was down inside me like a rock (p. 200); His silhouette was framed like a cardboard cutout against the burning flares (p. 211). See also pp. 208, 213. **Metaphors**—Jorgenson: pigeon (p. 204); O'Brien: the land, Nam, the horror, the war (p. 209). See also pp. 207, 211.

Pages 219–246

Rat Kiley shoots himself in the foot to escape active duty. O'Brien tells of the death of his childhood friend Linda.

Vocabulary

mutant (220) snipe hunt (221) protoplasm (221) ghoulish (222)
chronologies (228) illusion (230) inert (232) translucent (235)
blatant (239)

Acronyms

NVA (219)

Discussion Questions

1. Discuss what Rat Kiley does to escape active duty in Vietnam, why he does so, and what this signifies about the men in battle. *(What: He shoots himself in the foot and is airlifted back to base camp. Why: After hearing rumors of an enemy buildup in the area, the platoon begins to move only at night, trying to sleep in the daytime. The blackness of the nights and the fear of unseen danger cause the men severe emotional stress. Kiley, who has seen too many body bags and too much gore, breaks under the strain, talking nonstop about killer bugs, clawing at his skin, and hallucinating about the gory death of the other men. His actions signify the psychological toll of war, e.g., sleep deprivation, fear, deaths of others. The actions of others toward him after he shoots himself signify their camaraderie and compassion. pp. 219–224)*

2. Examine details about the old Vietnamese man's death. Elicit responses as to what this reveals about war. *(After a skirmish near a small village, Lt. Cross orders an air strike, and the men watch the village burn. They find the village deserted when they enter it except for the one old man. Beginning with Dave Jensen, the men go to the body, shake his hand, and say a few words to him.*

They prop the body against a fence, call him the guest of honor, and propose toasts to him. This happens on O'Brien's fourth day in the war, and the men's actions of greeting the dead make him nauseated. Kiowa sympathizes with him. Responses will vary. Ideas: The men develop various coping skills to help them survive the horrors of war. By treating the corpse as if it is alive, they mask the reality of death and cover their fears of their own mortality. War thus becomes a "game," rather than a matter of life and death. pp. 225–226)

3. Analyze why the old man's death triggers O'Brien's memories of Linda and why these memories are important to him. *(The man is his first encounter with death in Vietnam. Linda is his first encounter with death. Linda is nine, his first date, and they are in love. Their parents arrange for their chaperoned date. They talk very little and are awkward with each other. He remembers, and later regrets, making a stupid comment about her cap. The memories of Linda become interspersed with memories of Ted Lavender, the first member of his platoon to die in Vietnam. pp. 224–231)*

4. Analyze the importance of stories in O'Brien's memories of those who died. Note his statement, "We kept the dead alive with stories" (p. 239). *(He finds an illusion of aliveness in recalling stories about Linda and the others. By telling about his love for Linda, her illness, and her embarrassment when a boy pulls her cap from her almost-bald head, he creates an image of her for the reader and purges his conscience for failing to defend her. His story of Ted Lavender's death and the men's ensuing farewell conversation with Lavender temporarily bring him back to life. The story of Curt Lemon trick-or-treating at Halloween temporarily brings him back to life for the soldiers. In stories, miracles can happen, e.g., Linda smiles, sits up, talks to him, goes ice skating with him. pp. 230–242)*

5. Analyze what O'Brien means by the final statement, "I realize it is Tim trying to save Timmy's life with a story." *(Forty-three-year-old Tim O'Brien, the author, struggles with his own memories of the Vietnam War.* The Things They Carried, *with its separate but linked stories, is one way he deals with the emotional burdens he carries. Most of the stories are fiction with fragments of real events, yet they communicate the horror of the war and allow the author to deal with personal memories of the trauma and violence. Through the catharsis of words, Tim O'Brien tries to save his life, i.e., purge the memories from his mind and set himself, Timmy, free to live. p. 246)*

Supplementary Activities

1. Have students write a poem or short essay in which they (a) describe what they imagine it must be like to face the death of someone close to them or (b) relate a memory of someone who has died.

2. Have students add one simile and one metaphor to their list. **Simile**—It's (Kiley's visions of himself dead) like staring into this huge black crystal ball (p. 223). **Metaphor**—whole war: big banquet (p. 223)

Post-reading Discussion Questions

1. Using the graphic organizer on page 7 of this guide, characterize the fictitious Tim O'Brien. *(**Statements:** Speaking of the story about Lemon's death and the death of the water buffalo. "None of it happened. And even if it did happen, it didn't happen on the mountains, it happened in this little village on the Batangan Peninsula" [p. 85]. To Kathleen after placing Kiowa's moccasins in the field, "All that's finished" [p. 188]. **Behavior:** attempts to defect to Canada; sickened by death in Vietnam; struggles to find closure. **Fears:** being thought a coward; death. **Thoughts:** War is hell; but he also thinks it is mystery, terror, adventure, discovery, holiness, and a myriad of other emotions [p. 80]. Memories of smells, especially the field of human waste and mud, and the men who died and those who lived; plots revenge against Jorgenson. **Looks:** young, innocent. **Others' actions toward him:** respectful, supportive, occasionally mocking.)*

2. Using the graphic organizer on page 8 of this guide, characterize the major characters in the novel other than the narrator. *(Men of Alpha Company: Note that most of the men are 19–20 years old. **Jimmy Cross:** 24 years old, first lieutenant and platoon leader; feels responsible for his men, blames himself for each death; **Kiowa:** Native American, compassionate, devout Christian, narrator's close friend; **Mitchell Sanders:** kind and impartial, devoted to other soldiers; **Norman Bowker:** quiet, introspective, blames himself for Kiowa's death; **Azar:** cruel, unkind, makes crude jokes about death; **Ted Lavender:** terrified, often spaced out from drugs, first man to die; **Bob "Rat" Kiley:** brave, efficient platoon medic; **Curt Lemon:** brags, exaggerates, dies a horrible death)*

3. Using the graphic organizer on page 9 of this guide, summarize the novel. *(**Characters:** Main—Tim O'Brien [narrator], Jimmy Cross, Ted Lavender, Mitchell Sanders, Norman Bowker, "Rat" Kiley, Kiowa, Azar, Curt Lemon; Minor—Henry Dobbins, Dave Jensen, Lee Strunk, Elroy Berdahl, Mary Anne Bell, Mark Fossie, Kathleen. **Themes:** psychological stress, anxiety, shame/embarrassment, fear, guilt, blame, loneliness, survival, isolation, violence, truth, memory. **Setting:** Vietnam, United States. **Point of View:** primarily first-person with some stories in third person omniscient. **Genre:** fiction with some factual details. **Conflict:** United States vs. Viet Cong; person vs. self, person vs. person, person vs. Government. **Author's Style and Tone:** narrative; forthright.)*

4. Analyze the guilt/blame syndrome throughout the novel. *(Note the statement on page 177, "When a man died, there had to be blame." O'Brien: feels guilty for trying to defect to Canada yet blames himself for being weak and failing to do so. He feels guilty for causing Kiowa's death by revealing their location with a flashlight and blames himself for his death. He believes Jorgenson is guilty of negligence and blames him for almost allowing him to die. Jimmy Cross feels guilty for loving Martha more than the men in his platoon and blames himself for each death. He feels guilty for making his men build camp at the edge of the river and blames himself for Kiowa's death. Bowker feels guilty for releasing his hold on Kiowa's boot and blames himself for his death; thus, he also blames himself for not receiving the Silver Star.)*

5. Examine the symptoms of Post-Traumatic Stress Disorder (PTSD) and correlate with the post-war experiences of the men. *(This is a psychological illness in which people repeatedly relive, remember, and/or dream about a horrible experience. It may be called combat or battle fatigue for soldiers who experience this. Symptoms: flashbacks, repetitious dreams, vivid memories,*

sleeplessness, difficulty concentrating, and/or feelings of fear, anger, guilt, and helplessness. Those suffering from PTSD may feel emotionally numb and isolated from others. The symptoms may persist for several years. Student responses will vary. Ideas: O'Brien—flashbacks: Lavender's and Lemons' deaths; vivid memories, including smells and sights, e.g., Kiowa's death; dreams: death in Vietnam intermingled with Linda's death; Bowker—flashbacks; memories; guilt, e.g., Kiowa's death; emotional numbness and isolation, feels no one cares and no one is there to listen to him; Cross—anger; guilt, e.g. the deaths of his men.)

6. Elicit student responses as to how much of the book is totally fiction and how much is autobiographical. Ask students to cite specific examples from the book. *(Responses will vary. Have students note the message on the copyright page, "This is a work of fiction. Except for a few details regarding the author's own life, all the incidents, names, and characters are imaginary" and the story "Good Form" (pp. 179–180). Fact and fiction intermingle, and some stories are told and retold from different points of view. The narrator is Tim O'Brien, yet he acknowledges that many of the events in the stories did not really happen or, if they did happen, he changes details in different accounts of the same event. In "Good Form," O'Brien states that he is 43 years old, a writer, had been a foot soldier in Vietnam, was afraid to look at the dead bodies, and still feels grief and responsibility. According to information provided on the Amazon.com Web site, O'Brien did not attempt to defect to Canada, he never killed a man, and he does not have a daughter named Kathleen. Both the narrator Tim O'Brien and the author Tim O'Brien fought in a war in which they didn't believe and thought they were cowards for having done so.)*

7. Discuss why only one story, "The Man I Killed," completely focuses on a Vietnamese character. *(Responses will vary. Ideas: This story personalizes and reveals the horror of the war by revealing a soldier's personal reaction to one man among innumerable Vietnamese who were killed in the war. The majority of the book recounts stories about Americans who fought and died in Vietnam and the things they carried into the war and the things they brought home from the war. "The Man I Killed" could have been the story of any man who killed someone and then relived that moment again and again, questioning whether or not the death was necessary.)*

8. Discuss characters in the novel who engage in daydreams during and after the war and analyze why they do so. *(O'Brien—his life before Vietnam; people who have died come alive again: Linda, Kiowa, Lavender, Lemon; Cross—daydreams often about Martha, what she is doing, the two of them together, what he wishes they had done, and what they will do after the war; Bowker—talks to Sally Kramer Gustafson about the war; tells his dad why he didn't receive the Silver Star; relives the night Kiowa died. Responses will vary. Ideas: Their daydreams symbolize a coping mechanism through which the men relieve the monotony and tension of war, attempt to justify their actions in the war, attempt to find closure for the death of someone they loved, and try to explain to others what really happened in Vietnam.)*

9. Analyze why O'Brien includes the story of Mary Anne Bell in the novel. *(She symbolizes the deterioration war produces in the participants. By showing her transformation from innocence and beauty to hardness and cruelty, O'Brien reveals the effect war can have on anyone, regardless of age or sex. Just as Mary Anne becomes almost unrecognizable after getting a taste for war, those who fought often could not recognize themselves or anyone else in the aftermath of war. Mary Anne loses her identity and eventually joins the "missing," just as many veterans lost, at least for a time, their identity and joined the ranks of those searching for something to appease the pain.)*

10. Fill in the character chart on page 29 (1) a character's role in Alpha Company, (2) individual physical and emotional burdens, (3) his personal items, and (4) what happens to him. Using the overhead transparency, have students fill in the information. Note that they carried things essential for survival, "ghosts," emotional baggage such as grief and fear, cowardice, their own lives, and sometimes each other. *(Sample answer: Lt. Jimmy Cross, platoon leader—responsibility for the lives of his men, letters from and pictures of Martha; compass, maps, code books, binoculars, pistol, strobe light, good-luck pebble; survives)*

11. Reflect on the importance of Elroy Berdahl to Tim O'Brien. Discuss the significance of Berdahl's silence. If Berdahl had acted differently, how might it have affected O'Brien?

12. Using your own words, define the term "cowardice." Then decide whether or not you think O'Brien's decision to fight in the war was an act of cowardice.

Character Chart

Name and Role in Alpha Co.	Physical/Emotional Burdens He Carries	Personal Items He Carries	What Happens to Him

Post-reading Extension Activities

Note: The instructions for the extensions and assessment are directed toward the student.

1. Retell one character's story in a narrative poem of at least 24 lines.
2. Write a diamente poem contrasting one of the characters before and after the Vietnam War.
3. Write a eulogy for Kiowa.
4. Write a letter from Jimmy Cross to Kiowa's father explaining his death (see pp. 167–169).
5. Create a collage that symbolizes the various emotions the men of Alpha Company experience.
6. Prepare a montage of actual pictures from the Vietnam War.
7. Write and perform a ballad about Mary Anne Bell. Set the lyrics to a familiar tune, or create your own.
8. Prepare and present to the class a monologue in which you tell one version of Kiowa's death: Cross', Bowker's, or O'Brien's.
9. Interview a Vietnam War veteran and present your report to the class. This can be done via audio or video cassette or an oral report. Prepare a questionnaire before the interview.
10. Invite someone you know who has viewed the Vietnam Memorial to come and talk to the class, showing pictures if possible, and explaining his and others' personal reactions to the memorial.
11. Bring to class newspaper or magazine articles and pictures that relate to life in Vietnam today, as well as the current state of United States and Vietnam relations.
12. Research the development of the Vietnam War Memorial and select magazine and newspaper articles and pictures relating to the memorial. Display your articles and pictures as you present an oral report to the class.

Assessment for *The Things They Carried*

Assessment is an ongoing process. The following ten items can be completed during the novel study. Once finished, the student and teacher will check the work. Points may be added to indicate the level of understanding.

Name ______________________________ Date ______________

Student	Teacher	
______	______	1. Correct your unit quizzes, then discuss your answers with others in a small group.
______	______	2. Display or perform your extension project on the assigned day.
______	______	3. Write two review questions over the novel. As a class, conduct the review.
______	______	4. In a small group, prepare and conduct a panel discussion on the book. Choose panel members and write a series of questions for the audience.
______	______	5. Compare any literary analysis or comprehension graphics with members of a small group.
______	______	6. Write a name poem for one character from the book. Read your poem aloud and conduct a discussion about the character.
______	______	7. As your teacher calls out characters' names, write down the first word that comes to your mind about each character.
______	______	8. As your teacher writes the names of stories from the novel on the overhead transparency, participate in an oral discussion about what happened in each story.
______	______	9. Write a book review. Use at least ten of the vocabulary words from the novel.
______	______	10. Compare your completed lists of similes and metaphors in a small group.

Glossary

Pages 1–26

1. metabolism (2): the chemical process by which living things turn food into energy and living tissue
2. topography (5): the surface features of a region; ground
3. volition (15): act of willing; decision; choice
4. ambiguities (16): uncertainties; things that are vague or lack clarity
5. encyst (20): enclose
6. comport (25): conduct oneself in a certain manner

Pages 27–38

1. antipersonnel (36): directed against enemy troops
2. lethal (37): causing death; deadly; mortal

Pages 39–66

1. amortizing (40): setting aside something to accumulate interest for future settling of a debt
2. liberal (42): tolerant; now narrow in view; broad-minded
3. hawk (42): a person who advocates a warlike or military solution in conflict; warmonger
4. eviscerated (42): removed the bowels from
5. deferments (43): postponements; delays
6. pacifist (44): a person who is opposed to war and favors settling disputes by peaceful means
7. schizophrenia (44): a mental conflict showing marked inconsistencies or contradictions
8. acquiescence (45): quietly agreeing or submitting; consent
9. platitudes (45): dull or commonplace remarks; cliches
10. cryptic (49): having a hidden meaning; secret; ambiguous
11. reticence (51): tendency to say little; reserved
12. impassive (60): without feeling or emotion; unmoved

Pages 67–88

1. villes (68): cities (French)
2. rectitude (68): upright conduct or character; honesty

3. surreal (71): dreamlike distortion of reality; eerie; bizarre
4. napalm (75): a chemical substance that thickens gasoline, used in making fire bombs
5. ordnance (75): military weapons of all kinds
6. aesthetic (81): having to do with the beautiful or artful as distinguished from the useful, moral, or scientific
7. anarchy (82): disorder and confusion; lawlessness
8. trite (83): worn out by constant use or repetition; stale
9. sadism (87): practice of a person who gets pleasure from hurting someone else; unnatural love of cruelty

Pages 89–116

1. mundane (89): of this world; earthly; ordinary
2. superlatives (90): exaggerations; excesses
3. imprecision (99): inexactness; lack of accuracy
4. opaque (105): not letting light through
5. digressions (107): turning aside from main subject in writing or talking
6. endorphins (114): protein substances in the brain that suppress pain

Pages 117–136

1. eccentricity (117): something out of the ordinary; peculiarity; oddity
2. talisman (118): anything that acts as a magic token or charm
3. pagoda (119): temple or other sacred building
4. cadres (128): groups of trained men
5. piasters (129): unit of money in South Vietnam
6. hamlet (135): small village

Pages 137–161

1. affluent (138): having wealth; rich
2. valor (140): bravery; courage
3. irony (146): event or outcome which is the opposite of what is naturally expected; ambiguity
4. catharsis (157): purging; emotional purification

5. metaphoric (159): implying comparison between two different things
6. virtues (160): characteristics of moral excellence
7. anthology (160): collection of prose or poetry selections
8. complicity (160): partnership in wrongdoing; conspiracy

Pages 162–188

1. latrine (166): toilet or privy
2. tactically (169): skillfully; strategically planning the direction of military forces in a battle
3. elusive (170): evasive; tending to escape
4. condolences (176): expressions of sympathy

Pages 189–218

1. gangrene (190): decay and death of tissue when blood supply is obstructed
2. tempo (193): pace; rhythm
3. tic (201): habitual, involuntary twitching of muscles, especially of the face
4. levitate (202): rise or float in the air
5. rapport (203): connection; agreement; harmony
6. coherence (209): act of sticking together; tendency to hold together
7. atrocity (209): very great wickedness or cruelty
8. resonance (210): resounding quality; impressive; striking
9. inflection (212): change in tone or pitch of the voice
10. wistful (212): longing; yearning
11. lucid (214): clear in intellect; sane; rational

Pages 219–246

1. mutant (220): a new genetic character or variety of plant or animal resulting from alteration
2. snipe hunt (221): a prank played on a person by inviting him to a desolate place to hunt "snipe" with others who never come
3. protoplasm (221): living matter
4. ghoulish (222): revolting; brutally horrible
5. chronologies (228): arrangements of exact dates of events in order in which they appear

6. illusion (230): false impression or perception; delusion
7. inert (232): having no power to move or act; lifeless
8. translucent (235): transparent; letting light through
9. blatant (239): obviously outrageous

Acronyms

1. SOP (2): Standard Operating Procedure
2. RTO (3): Radio Telephone Operator
3. PRC (5): Portable Radio Communications
4. PFC (5): Private First Class
5. KIA (6): Killed in Action
6. AO (9): Area of Operations
7. USO (14): United Services Operation
8. AWOL (35): Absent Without Leave
9. SEATO (40): Southeast Asia Treaty Organization
10. CO (44): Conscientious Objector
11. FBI (50): Federal Bureau of Investigation
12. LZ (62): Landing Zone
13. LP (72): Listening Post
14. VC (78): Viet Cong
15. NCO (91): Non-Commissioned Officer
16. RF (91): Regional Forces
17. PF (91): Popular Forces
18. ARVN (91): Army of the Republic of Vietnam
19. R&R (113): Rest and Recreation
20. MP (115): Military Police
21. CID (115): Criminal Investigation Department
22. GI (145): Government Issue

23. MIA (163): Missing in Action
24. LT (166): Lieutenant
25. NVA (219): North Vietnamese Army

Military/Slang Terms

1. rucksack (1): infantryman's backpack
2. foxhole (1): protective hole in the ground big enough for one or two people
3. fatigue (2): combat uniform
4. flak jacket (3): protective vest
5. to hump (3): walk, march
6. grunts (5): an infantry man in the U.S. military
7. platoon (5): subdivision of large military unit
8. Toe Poppers, Bouncing Betties (9): mines
9. Poppa-san (33): older Vietnamese man
10. dink (33), gook (67): derogatory terms for foreigners, especially Asians
11. body bag (37): plastic bag for dead bodies
12. dustoff (66): medical evacuation by helicopter
13. boonies (90): jungle or swampy areas
14. Green Berets (92): U.S. Special Forces
15. Ruff-and-Puffs (91): slang term for Regional and Popular Forces
16. Mama-san (93): older Vietnamese woman
17. *didi mau* (122): Vietnamese slang for "go quickly"
18. stand-down (193): return of infantry unit to base camp
19. klicks (195): kilometers
20. Charlie Cong (202): Viet Cong, i.e., the enemy
21. bunker (204): fortified shelter beneath the ground